# The Man on the Mountain Top

## In Search of the Truth about Noah

### Nick Thom

Published by

**Dayglo Books Ltd, Nottingham, UK**

info@dayglobooks.co.uk

0004-14-1602-13

© Nick Thom 2014

The right of Nick Thom to be identified as the author of this work has been asserted by him in accordance with the Designs and Copyright Act 1988.

Artwork & illustrations by
www.valentineart.co.uk
Cover design by Madeleine Tighe

Typeset in Opendyslexic

by Abelardo Gonzalez (2011)

Printed by IngramSpark

Distributed by Filament Publishing Ltd

This book is subject to international copyright and may not be copied in any way without the prior written permission of the publishers.

**The Story of Noah and the Ark**

from the Authorised Version of the Bible, printed in 1611 – Genesis, chapters 6-9:

'And God said unto Noah: "The end of all flesh is come before me; for the earth is filled with violence; and behold, I will destroy the earth.

"Make thee an ark of gopher wood; rooms shalt thou make in the ark, and shalt pitch it within and without with pitch.

"And this is the fashion which thou shalt make it of: The length of the ark shall be three hundred cubits, the breadth of it fifty cubits, and the height of it thirty cubits.

"A window shalt thou make to the ark; and a door shalt thou set in the side thereof; with lower, second and third stories shalt thou make it.

"And behold, I, even I, do bring a flood of waters upon the earth, to destroy all flesh, wherein is the breath of life; and everything that is in the earth shall die.

"But with thee will I establish my covenant; and thou shalt come into the ark, thou, and thy sons, and thy wife, and thy sons' wives with thee.

"And of every living thing of all flesh, two of every sort shalt thou bring into the ark, to keep them alive with thee; they shall be male and female.

"Of fowls, and of cattle, and of every creeping thing of the earth after its kind, two of every sort shall come unto thee, to keep them alive.

"And take thou unto thee of all food that is eaten, for thee and for them."

Thus did Noah; according to all that God commanded him.

And the Lord said unto Noah: "I will cause it to rain upon the earth forty days and forty nights; and every living substance that I have made will I destroy from off the face of the earth."

In the selfsame day entered Noah into the ark, and every beast went in, as God had commanded him, and the Lord shut him in.

And the flood was forty days upon the earth; and the waters increased and bore up the ark and it was lifted up above the earth.

And the waters increased greatly upon the earth; and the ark went upon the face of the waters.

And the waters prevailed exceedingly upon the earth; and all the high hills that were under the whole heaven, were covered.

Fifteen cubits upward did the waters prevail; and the mountains were covered.

And all flesh died that moved upon the earth, both of fowl, and of cattle, and of beast, and every creeping thing upon the earth, and every man.

All in whose nostrils was the breath of life, of all that was on the dry land, died.

And every living substance was destroyed which was upon the face of the ground; and Noah only remained alive, and they that were with him in the ark.

And the waters prevailed upon the earth a hundred and fifty days.

And God remembered Noah, and made a wind to pass over the earth, and the waters reduced. The windows of heaven were stopped, and the rain was restrained.

The waters returned from off the earth and after the hundred and fifty days the waters abated.

And the ark rested, in the seventh month, upon the mountains of Ararat.

And the waters decreased continually until the tenth month. In the tenth month, on the first day of the month, were the tops of the mountains seen.

At the end of forty days, Noah opened the window and sent forth a raven which went forth to and fro, until the waters were dried up from off the earth.

Also he sent forth a dove, to see if the waters were abated; but the dove found no rest for the sole of her foot, and she returned unto him into the ark.

Noah stayed another seven days and again he sent forth the dove; and the dove came to him in the evening; and lo, in her mouth was an olive leaf plucked off, so Noah knew that the waters were abated from off the earth.

And Noah removed the covering of the ark and looked, and, behold, the face of the ground was dry.

Noah went forth with his sons and his wife and his sons' wives. Every beast, every creeping thing and every fowl, after their kinds, went forth out of the ark.

And God blessed Noah and his sons and said unto them: "Be fruitful, and multiply, and replenish the earth.

"And I will establish my covenant with you; I do set my bow in the cloud, and it shall be for a token of a covenant between me and you and every living creature, for perpetual generations; and the waters shall no more become a flood to destroy all flesh."'

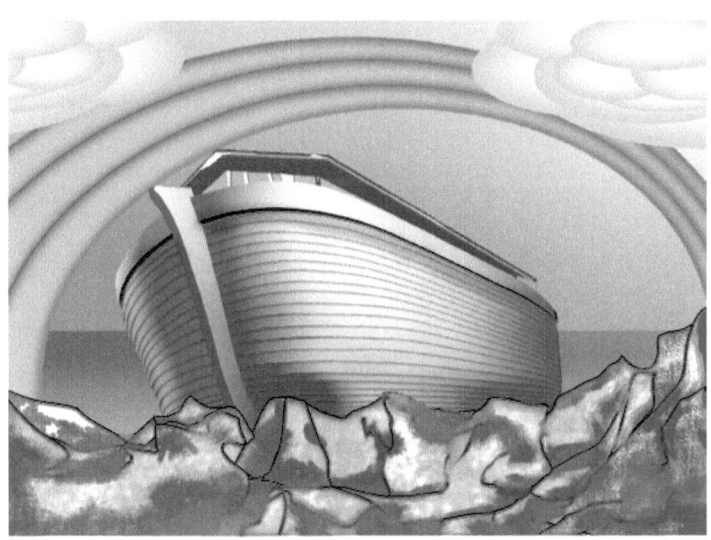

# The Man on the Mountain Top

**CHAPTER 1     FLOODS AND GREAT FLOODS**

The story of Noah has long caught the imagination – hence the large number of books and films that have been produced on the subject. Yet few scientists would credit it with more than the smallest grain of truth.

After all, who can say they have seen a flood that covered a mountain?

True, we have lived through remarkable events like the tsunamis that struck the countries around the Indian Ocean in 2004 and Japan in 2011.

We watched while Hurricane Katrina submerged most of the city of New Orleans. There seem to be massive river floods in one part of the world or another every year.

In the UK we were rather taken aback when a large chunk of the county of Somerset lay underwater for many weeks in the winter of 2013-2014.

But set against the story of Noah these are trifling affairs; barely deep enough to float an ark let alone to strand it on the top of a mountain!

So the question I want to ask is: could Noah's flood really have happened?

And if so, when? How deep? And what on earth could have caused it? These are big questions – but I hope you will come to see that they do indeed have answers.

Right now, if you ask most scientists, or for that matter scholars of the Bible, for their best explanation, you are likely to get one of three responses:

1) It is simply the distant memory of the rise of the oceans after the Ice Age.

2) It stems from the so-called 'Black Sea flood' (proposed by Bill Ryan and Walter Pitman in their book 'Noah's Flood'). The waters of the Mediterranean are supposed to have burst through the Bosphorus channel –

where Istanbul is today – and into the basin of the Black Sea.

3) It was just a very large river flood, either of the Tigris or the Euphrates rivers, or both. These rivers flow from Turkey through Iraq, where the story of Noah is set.

But all three explanations have some pretty serious problems.

Firstly, the rate of sea level rise at the end of the Ice Age was never more than about two metres in a human lifetime – that's as quick as it ever got.

If that's a 'great flood' then our ancestors must have been pretty easily scared, as well as having a serious tendency to exaggerate!

Set against this, the Black Sea flood seems really quite a good solution.

It is supposed to have happened about 8,000 years ago and it would have been much more dramatic. There are estimates of a foot or two of sea level rise per day across a wide plain along the northern shore of the sea.

One problem is that it's in the wrong place. The story in the Bible is set in Iraq, not around the Black Sea coasts.

Another is that a majority of scientists reckon the theory has been disproved and the Black Sea flood simply never happened.

So that leaves the river flood theory.

The early stories of the Bible are set in Iraq, the land through which two mighty rivers flow. They carry rainfall run-off and snow melt from the mountains of eastern Turkey all the way to the Persian Gulf.

It was here in 1929, whilst excavating the southern Iraqi city of Ur, that the famous archaeologist Leonard Woolley found evidence for a very substantial flood.

He dug down through the layers of Ur's royal history, the so-called Early Dynastic period ($3^{rd}$ millennium BC). Then he dug down through earlier, pre-Dynastic layers. Then entered solid clay.

It looked as though the earliest days of Ur's history had been reached.

However, Woolley was not convinced.

He instructed his diggers to keep on going. They removed eight feet – 2.5 metres – of clay and then, suddenly, they found another city layer.

It was quite different in character from the layers above the clay. The pottery was different and the buildings were constructed differently.

It suggested that Ur had been abandoned for a period and then rebuilt at a later date, possibly by quite different people.

And since the clay could only have been deposited by water, this meant that the city of Ur had been engulfed by a very serious flood, probably some time around 3,800 BC.

Could this have been the flood of Noah?

---

      archaeology ✓    geography ✓   creatures
  science    language    religion ✓  folklore

# CHAPTER 2            ESSENTIAL POINTS

Woolley's findings from elsewhere on the site of Ur were less widely publicised.

From the higher part of the city, in contrast to lower down, there was absolutely no clay layer at all. The 'occupation' layers simply followed one from another.

This could only mean that this particular flood, though spectacular, had a limited depth.

Nevertheless, the flood would have covered a very wide area indeed. In fact, from the high vantage point of Ur's citadel, the entire land would have appeared to be underwater.

It is easy to see how such a devastating flood could lead to tales of high drama and spectacular escape.  The flood would have been a genuinely sudden event and many people would certainly have lost their lives.

Escape by boat would have been a logical and sensible course of action, So it is not hard to see the story of Noah emerging from the flood waters.

Yet it can hardly be said to have covered mountains! If it was the source of the Noah story, then that story has certainly grown in the telling.

So let's take a closer look at the story of Noah – a story that is given in both the Bible and the Koran. The essential points are:

- Noah was warned by God to build a boat – the ark – to escape a flood.
- He took his family on board, together with representatives of different types of animal.
- The flood came, by rain and also by the sea rising.
- Everyone on earth apart from Noah died.
- The tops of the mountains were covered.
- The flood lasted several months.
- The ark grounded in the mountains of Ararat, in eastern Turkey.

As I am sure you can see straight away, there are several features here that are quite different from any of the floods mentioned so far.

That doesn't prove anything on its own. Folk stories always tend to be embroidered by those telling them, but it should make us pause for thought.

The exaggeration seems to be so large. It takes the story far outside the bounds of normal imagination. One wonders how the key writings of three of our greatest religions – Judaism, Christianity and Islam – could have swallowed it.

How, for example, could anyone imagine that Noah ran aground amongst mountains to the north of the Iraqi plain? The rivers flow the other way!

What should we understand by the statement that the sea rose, as well as rain falling?

Let me immediately start to annoy some people. Some people are convinced that nothing is acceptable but a flood in which every creature on the planet died (except Noah and those with him).

I am quite prepared to accept less. I have no fixed agenda – I simply want to know the truth.

I am also not of the view that the right approach to solving the mystery of the Great Flood is to head off to the slopes of Mount Ararat, in eastern Turkey.

I may not be a Biblical scholar. But I know enough to realise that the text speaks of 'mountains' – not 'one mountain'. I also understand that the name 'Ararat' comes from 'Urartu'. That is the land which is now Kurdistan.

The description of Noah's landing place – whether it is true or false – could therefore refer to anywhere among the hills immediately north of the Iraqi plain.

The approach that I wish to take here is rather more scientific.

If there really was a flood like the one described in the Bible, then there will be evidence – genuine scientific evidence.

However, before bringing science to bear, I think we should first listen to the evidence of history.

The Bible story of Noah is probably the best known flood story from ancient times. But it is just one of countless folk memories – real or imagined – of peoples right across the planet.

This, therefore, is the logical place to start. There's an awful lot of folk history out there. Some of it might help us to get a better idea of what we are looking for.

I trust you'll find this journey of discovery an interesting one. Perhaps it will even prove a bit of an eye-opener.

It concerns the very distant past. It also concerns the trustworthiness of the Bible. By extension it also concerns the trustworthiness of the Koran, which clearly supports the Bible story.

The world deserves to know the truth, whatever that truth may be.

**CHAPTER 3**                  **HISTORY AND MYTH**

Back in the 19th Century much of archaeology was aimed directly at supporting the pages of the Bible – or at least illuminating them.

Some clay tablets covered with cuneiform writing were found in the ruins of the great northern Iraqi city of Nineveh. When the story broke that one of these tablets actually described a great flood, public excitement could hardly be contained.

The tablet concerned was actually part of a Bronze Age classic story, the 'Epic of Gilgamesh'. This was the most famous tale to emerge from ancient Iraq.

It was a best-seller throughout the 2nd millennium BC. Copies or part-copies have turned up in excavations from Egypt to Turkey, as well as in Iraq itself.

It had a similar status to the writings of Homer in later Greek society.

It's a fascinating and delightful story, well worth a read if you get a chance.

One key episode concerns a meeting that took place between Gilgamesh and a very old man called Utan-apishtim.

Gilgamesh had had a roller-coaster of a life. Following the death of his close friend Enkidu, his roller-coaster had just about left the tracks.

Once, he had been young, brash and confident, without a care in the world.

He was, after all, king of the powerful southern Iraqi city of Uruk. He had been successful in securing the supremacy of Uruk over the rival city of Kish, in central Iraq.

But now, following Enkidu's death, he had come face to face with his own mortality and it frightened him out of his wits!

He simply had to know the answer to life, the universe and everything.

There was only one man on earth who could possibly help. That was Utan-apishtim. According to the story this man had actually survived the flood.

So Gilgamesh set out on his long, hard, and geographically uncertain journey to meet Utan-apishtim. Eventually he found him.

Utan-apishtim then tells the story of the flood from his perspective. The essentials are as follows:

- The gods told him to build a ship.
- He took his family, some selected craftsmen, and representatives of the animal kingdom.
- The flood came with a seven-day storm.
- One or two islands were visible to Utan-apishtim during his time on board.
- Everyone apart from Utan-apishtim and his companions died in the flood.
- He eventually ran aground on Mount Nisir. Its location is unknown but it is said to be in Kurdistan or Armenia.

It's pretty much the same story as that of Noah!

The parallels are unmistakable. I could have added others, notably the fact that both Noah and Utan-apishtim are reported to have sent out birds to search for dry land. It was a raven and a dove in both stories, also a swallow in the case of Utan-apishtim.

From the texts alone, it's impossible to judge which is the more reliable version. But the two stories certainly derive from the same original. One wonders what the truth of that original may have been.

So can we date the Epic of Gilgamesh? The texts currently in our possession were written in the Akkadian language. This was the number one language of Iraq over a period of 2,000 years. They date from the mid $2^{nd}$ millennium BC onwards.

However the tale itself is set in much earlier times.

The picture painted is of a time when Uruk was rivalled by the city of Kish, lying some 100 miles to the north-west, up the river Euphrates.

This places the tale in the archaeological phase known as 'Early Dynastic One', with a date somewhere in the 2,800-2,500 BC range.

We also have a document known as the 'Sumerian king list', which is a list of the rulers of southern Iraq. This land was known in earliest times as 'Sumer'.

The fifth ruler listed in the '1$^{st}$ Dynasty of Uruk', bears the name Gilgamesh. So it all ties in nicely.

The problem is, finding a date for Gilgamesh does not date the flood.

Utan-apishtim is portrayed as a very old man indeed.

His life had been unnaturally extended by the gift of immortality. It sounds as though Utan-apishtim's flood was already a distant folk memory in Gilgamesh's day.

All of this means that Noah's flood remains a mystery.

The tale is old – very old indeed. It is much older than all the written texts we now possess, including the Epic of Gilgamesh.

And the type of flood which is described is quite unlike any that we experience today. It is striking in its duration. It lasted for months in the case of the Bible story.

It is remarkable in its depth. Mountains are covered. And there is the puzzling claim that the survivors grounded their ship on a mountain top!

It could be a complete invention, of course.

But it is not a Jewish, Christian or Muslim invention. Whether true or false, the origin of the story pre-dates all these religions.

But, as I said at the end of the last chapter, the story of Noah – or Utan-apishtim – is far from alone.

The truth is that large numbers of other flood stories can be found in tribal folklore from right across the face of the planet.

They may not be so well known. They are all stories that have been handed down orally. They will inevitably contain much that is the product of generations of fertile imagination.

However, the stories themselves are real enough. There is an absolutely consistent theme right across the world that one day, a very long time ago, water rose to an unprecedented height and covered the land.

## CHAPTER 4      STORIES FROM THE AMERICAS

Let me take you straight to the New World now. Here, there are eight versions of the same story, which I call 'The old man and the muskrat'.

I think this version will give you the general picture. It is from the Chippewa people. They live on the USA-Canada border, not far from Lake Superior:

"In the beginning of time, in September, there was a great snow. A mouse nibbled a hole in a leather bag which contained the sun's heat. The heat escaped and melted the snow in an instant.

The waters rose to cover even the highest mountains.

One old man had foreseen the flood and warned everybody. Others had thought to escape to the hills but they drowned in the flood.

The old man had prepared a canoe and survived, rescuing animals he came across.

After a while he sent in turn the beaver, otter, muskrat and duck to find land.

Only the duck returned, with some mud in its bill. The old man cast the mud on the water and blew on it, making solid land."


This tale is told across much of Canada, from Quebec to the Arctic Circle.

The essential features are that the old man rescues certain animals, that one of them (most commonly the muskrat) successfully dives for mud, and that the man then creates dry land by breathing on the mud.

Of course, I am not trying to make out that the details are true.

I just want you to notice that here is a flood, not unlike Noah's flood, and it's on the other side of the world!

Let me pluck another tale from the rich and varied collection of South American stories. This one is from the Purus River in central Amazonia:

"Once upon a time, people heard a rumbling above and below the ground. The sun and moon turned red, blue and yellow, and wild beasts mingled fearlessly with man.

A month later they saw darkness ascending from the earth to the sky. It was accompanied by a roar of thunder and heavy rain.

Everything was in dreadful confusion. Some people lost themselves. Some people died without knowing why.

The water rose to cover the earth, and people took refuge in the highest trees. There they perished from cold and hunger. It continued to be dark and rainy.

Only U-assu and his wife survived. When they came down after the flood they could not find even a sign of a single corpse."

Maybe in this case the depth of the flood was more limited. According to this story, drowning could be avoided simply by taking to the trees. However, starvation was then the threat, which implies a long-lasting event.

Again, it's not the details that are important.

It's the fact that the story exists at all. Once again, it speaks of a pretty spectacular flood.

---

| archaeology | geography | creatures |
| science | language | religion | folklore ✓ |

**CHAPTER 5**         **STORIES FROM ELSEWHERE**

To Australia next.

The aborigines are believed to have been cut off from the rest of the world for tens of thousands of years until Europeans arrived in the 18th Century. Here is one of their stories:

"A man's two wives ran away from him. He pursued them to Encounter Bay, saw them at a distance, and angrily cried out for the waters to rise and drown them.

A terrible flood washed over the hills and killed the two women. The waters rose so high that a man named Nepelle, who lived at Rauwoke, had to drag his canoe up to the top of the hill, now called Point Macleay.

The dense part of the Milky Way shows his canoe floating in the sky."

It's pretty mythical-sounding. All the Australian tales are. But here too we find an impossibly massive flood.

And if we cross to the mainland of south-east Asia the picture is the same. You can see this in this tale from the Burma-India border region:

"The king of the water demons fell in love with the woman Ngai-ti. She rejected him and ran away. He pursued her and surrounded the whole human race with water on the hill Phun-lu-buk, said to be in the far north-east.

Threatened by waters which continued to rise, the people threw Ngai-ti into the flood, which then receded."

This brings me to one of my favourite flood myths, the brother-sister story.

It is told by communities from central India to Taiwan and the Philippines.

On the Chinese island of Hainan it has become much more than a myth. It has developed into a traditional festival when young people get together and seek out future marriage partners.

Here is the version told by the Lisu people who live on the Burma-China border:

"After death came into the world as a result of a curse, sky and earth longed for human souls and bones. That is how the flood began.

An orphaned brother and sister lived in squalor in a village.

A pair of golden birds flew down to them one day. They warned them that a huge wave would flood the earth.

They told them to take shelter in a gourd and not to come out until they heard the birds again.

The two children warned their neighbours, but the people didn't believe them. The children sawed off the top of a gourd and went inside.

For ninety-nine days there was no wind or rain and the earth became parched. Then torrents of rain fell and the resulting flood washed everything away.

The brother and sister occasionally could hear the gourd bump against the bottom of heaven.

After long waiting, they heard the birds calling. They left the gourd and found they had landed atop a mountain, and the flood had receded.

The brother and sister then went in search of other people, exploring north and south respectively. They found nobody else.

The golden birds appeared again and urged them to marry. They refused. Then they consented. They had six sons and six daughters."

This version includes pretty much all the essential elements of the story.

It tells of a massive flood, seemingly hundreds of metres deep; escape by the brother and sister in some sort of floating vessel; a long time adrift; and that the two had to marry each other because there was no one else alive. Other details vary.

Here is one of the Indian tales:

"A boy and a girl were born to the first man and woman. God sent a deluge to destroy a jackal that had angered him.

The man and woman heard it coming. They shut their children in a hollow piece of wood with provisions to last until the flood subsided.

The deluge came and everything on earth was drowned. After 12 years God created two birds and sent them to see if the jackal had been drowned.

They saw nothing but a floating log. They landed on it and heard the children inside. They were saying to each other that they had only three days of provisions left.

The birds told God, who caused the flood to subside. He took the children from the log, and heard their story. In due time they were married."

And from Taiwan:

"In an earthquake, mountains tumbled down, the earth gaped and hot subterranean waters gushed out and flooded the whole earth.

Two sisters and a brother escaped in a wooden mortar and floated south to Rarauran. They landed and climbed Mount Kaburugan to view the countryside. Then the sisters searched south, and the brother searched west for good land.

Finding none, they returned and ascended to the mountain's summit again. Halfway up, the older sister tired. When the other two returned for her, they found she had turned into a rock.

They were uncertain whether it would be proper for them to marry. They asked the sun as it rose the next morning. The sun answered immediately that they may marry."

What makes this group of stories so fascinating is not the tale itself — although it's a good one – but the fact that they are so widely spread.

The stories cut across different ethnic groups and six different language families.

So let's dig a little deeper.

## CHAPTER 6  LANGUAGE AND THE FLOOD

Actually, only one language family spans all the lands where the brother-sister story is told. It is called Austro-Asiatic.

The Indian stories are from tribal peoples living in, or close to, Austro-Asiatic speaking parts of India.

Austro-Asiatic languages are still spoken in the border region between China, Burma and Thailand, as well as Vietnam.

These languages, in turn, are known to have had a strong influence on another group of languages known as Austro-nesian.

These are the languages of the tribes responsible for the two brother-sister stories from Taiwan.

The tale from the Philippines is from the Ifugao people who also speak an Austro-nesian language. This language originated prior to about 3,500 BC in Taiwan.

The inhabitants of the Chinese island of Hainan may well have suffered as much Austro-Asiatic language influence as people in Taiwan.

So it seems to me, that the history of the brother-sister is intimately tied in with the history of the Austro-Asiatic language family. Therefore it is potentially intimately tied in with the history of the flood itself. Are you still with me? I hope so.

The problem is that the history of this Austro-Asiatic language family is quite unknown.

Until the relationship between the Austro-Asiatic languages of India and the rest of the family was proven, linguists speculated about an origin in Central or Northern Asia.

This idea was based on similarities between the Indian Austro-Asiatic languages and the Uralic languages of Russia.

Despite the fact that this line of thought is out of fashion nowadays, my own studies have led me to agree with it.

I suggest that Austro-Asiatic languages entered Pakistan, and then India, from the northwest in about 9,000 BC. They would have reached the upland region of east-central India by about 6,500 BC.

From there, Austro-Asiatic languages exploded across south-east Asia. This was almost certainly on the back of the newly-developed skill of boat craft.

But if the brother-sister story was indeed spread by Austro-Asiatic speakers, and if these dates are true, then this pushes the origin of the story right back to 6,500 BC or shortly after. That is the date when the languages started to separate.

And this brings me to the most remarkable feature of the Austro-Asiatic language. This is a feature that I have not seen in any other language family on the planet.

There is a seemingly inexplicable difference in grammar between the languages of central India and those of the rest of the family.

It is a much greater difference than would be expected based on a comparison of vocabulary alone.

In fact, the difference is so great that it is as if one side of the family or the other sat down one day and completely re-designed the structure of their language. And for some reason they decided to model it on that of their neighbours, who spoke languages of the family known as Sino-Tibetan!

Yet, fascinatingly, this sort of thing can actually happen. It occurs when two peoples are thrust together and are forced to communicate.

Then, the resulting language is known as a 'pidgin'.

Pidgins arose all over the world as a result of the slave trade.

Slaves from different nations were forced to work together, so they had to communicate. They did their best with a combination of one another's languages. Their children then continued to use the somewhat artificial form of language their parents had resorted to.

But why should an Austro-Asiatic speaking group of people have felt such pressing need to communicate with a Sino-Tibetan group? This would be at a date which, in my assessment, fell some time between 6,500 BC and 6,000 BC.

What sort of emergency could have caused it?

And how was it that this particular community were the ones that then spread their culture like wildfire across the whole of south-east Asia? They could hardly have been slaves.

If the whole idea wasn't so ridiculous you would have to think that they were survivors of some terrible disaster. Maybe a disaster that forced two peoples to share the same refuge.

For example, an ever-shrinking patch of high ground, surrounded by rising flood waters.

Honestly, I am not making this up!

This unusual language difference is real –
and everything real has a real cause.

---

archaeology     geography     creatures
science     language ✓     religion     folklore

**CHAPTER 7**          **THE SAME THE WORLD OVER**

If that real cause was, in fact, a flood, then we can read about it in literally hundreds more folk tales.

The following map shows the 189 tales that I find credible and understandable. That is to say, not so mythical as to be absurd.

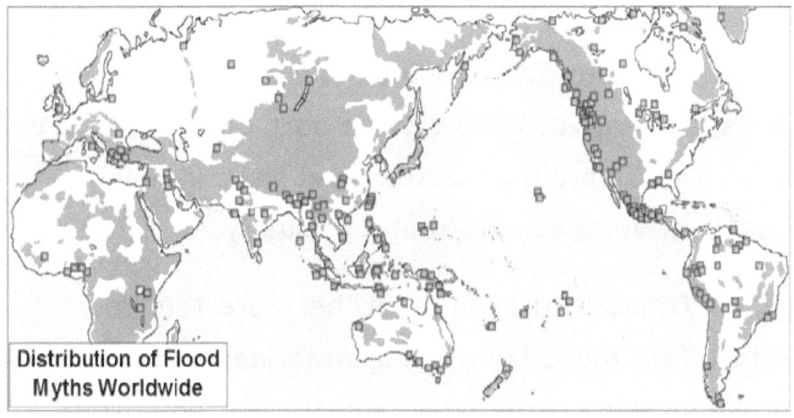

Distribution of Flood Myths Worldwide

There are obvious concentrations – notably America, South-East Asia and Australia.

There are also obvious gaps, notably much of Europe and Africa (I promise, there are none hidden by the title box).

We are left with two possible explanations.

The first is that the concept of a 'great flood' is so firmly embedded in the human race that it naturally springs up all over the world.

Or, there actually was some real and nearly worldwide event which triggered the various stories still told today.

I am no psychologist, but the first of these options doesn't seem all that likely to me.

And then there is the strange fact that it always seems to be the same sort of flood. There is an impossibly high water level that, in many cases, developed relatively gradually.

To illustrate the point, here are four more tales. Two more from North America; the Hindu story of Manu, from India; and the ancient Greek story of Deucalion:

1) "As the tide rose and touched the woman's feet, she moved up a little and sat down again. The tide kept rising, following the woman.

The villagers soon became alarmed at its unprecedented height. Having no canoes, they prepared rafts and provisioned them with fish and water.

At last the tide covered the whole island. The people saved themselves on rafts."


2) "When the Squamish saw the great flood coming, they held a council and decided to make a giant canoe.

The men worked day and night to make this canoe, the biggest ever. The women made a long rope of oiled cedar fibres with which they tied the canoe to a giant rock.

They put every baby into the canoe with food and water. They selected the bravest young man and the mother of the youngest baby to go as their guardians.

No one cried as the waters rose and drowned everyone else.

After several days the man saw a speck far to the south. By the next day he could see that it was a mountain top, Mount Baker. He cut the rope and paddled to it, and made a new home there."


3) "Manu, the first human, found a small fish in his washwater. The fish begged protection from the larger fishes, in return for which it would save Manu. Manu kept the fish safe. He transferred it to larger and larger containers as it grew. Eventually he took it to the ocean.

The fish warned Manu of a coming deluge and told him to build a ship. When the flood rose, the fish came and Manu tied the craft to its horn.

The fish led him to a northern mountain and told Manu to tie the ship's rope to a tree to prevent it from drifting. Manu alone of all creatures survived."

4) "Zeus sent a flood to destroy the men of the Bronze Age. Prometheus advised his son Deucalion to build a chest. All other men perished except for a few who escaped to high mountains.

The mountains in Thessaly were parted. All the world beyond the isthmus and the Peloponnese was overwhelmed.

Deucalion and his wife Pyrrha floated in the chest for nine days and nights. Then they landed on Parnassus. When the rains ceased, he sacrificed to Zeus, the god of escape."


I know the last example speaks of the Bronze Age, which didn't start until about 3,000 BC, but I wouldn't get too hung up on that.

There is, as it happens, a story from Central Asia that speaks of iron. Details will never be reliable. In the case of Deucalion's flood, the point is that the story applied to a past age.

Anyway, I think we have seen enough.

What stands out is that an awful lot of peoples from different corners of the world tell a story of a time when the waters rose to cover the land.

In many cases it is clearly stated that the sea rose. In other cases a lake rose, or the waters are said to have sprung from the earth.

This is the sort of thing people who had never seen the sea would say, even if the sea was actually the real source of the water.

In most cases no explanation is given. But if it's true – if the sea really did rise to cover the land – how on earth could it have happened?

The mind boggles – which means we are tempted to dismiss it completely.

But should we?

---

    archaeology    geography    creatures
    science    language    religion    folklore ✓

**CHAPTER 8                    OUR WOBBLY PLANET**

You can't really judge from the stories just how deep this flood was.

Noah is said to have landed in the 'mountains of Ararat'. But, as I said, that could mean anywhere in the hills north of the Iraqi plain. Nevertheless, even in the foothills we are talking of a 300 metre rise in sea level!

There are about 1,300 million cubic kilometres of water in the oceans today.

A 300 metre flood would require another 130 million or so – an extra 10%. That's a lot of water.

From a rational point of view there is only one possible source for flood water on this scale. It must have come from the oceans themselves.

In theory, if the oceans somehow redistributed themselves, then you could end up with dramatic sea level rises in one part of the world and dramatic falls in other parts.

That is what we see today in the tides, which are caused by the moon's pull on the Earth. When it's high tide in New York, it's low tide in Ireland.

The total volume of water stays the same, but what we see on the shore changes.

The problem is the moon couldn't pull any more than it does at the moment.

Even if some other heavenly body passed by, causing much greater pull, the tides would still operate on a twice daily cycle, and that simply doesn't match the stories.

But there is another sort of tide. You may never have heard of it, and I'm sure you have never noticed it. Its technical name is a 'pole tide' and it's miniscule.

It is caused by a slight wobble of the Earth such that the North and South poles shift by up to about six metres over a 14-month cycle.

Scientists still debate the exact reason for the wobble. But it definitely means that the planet is slightly out of balance.

One reason could be snow falling and remaining frozen, and then melting months later. Another could be the oceans expanding in volume when they warm, and then shrinking slightly when they cool.

Basically, this wobble is not a big deal. But what if the Earth experienced something that really threw it out of balance?

Our planet is not a very stable structure. It's full of magma lakes and faults, like the San Andreas Fault in California. Not to mention the fact that the whole mantle is supported by nothing more than a sea of liquid iron!

It really doesn't take a lot to generate a wobble. A wobble will always generate a tide. The shape of the Earth means that the land will do something different from the oceans.

The problem is, that to create a 300 metre pole tide the Earth would have to wobble by about 6 degrees.

That would mean a 400-mile shift in the location of the North and South poles – which is a lot.

But, just over 8,000 years ago, in about 6,250 BC, something really did throw the Earth out of balance.

At the end of the last Ice Age in about 9,500 BC, the glaciers in North America began melting.

As they melted, a lake formed at their base. The further northwards the glaciers retreated, the more the lake at their feet expanded.

The glaciers acted as a dam, holding in the water.

As the lake got bigger and bigger, it was sandwiched between the ice dam of the glacier and a ridge of high ground in the middle of the North American continent.

Scientists call it Lake Agassiz.

When fully grown, it was immense. It was much bigger than any lake today, including the Caspian Sea, which is the biggest lake on the planet. Imagine Italy . . . The Caspian Sea is bigger!

When the ice dam finally gave way, the whole lot suddenly drained out into the oceans.

In the course of approximately 6 months, this is what happened. Over 150,000 cubic kilometres of water disappeared from North America and redistributed itself across the oceans of the world.

That's 150 trillion tonnes suddenly not there any more.

The earth would have been seriously out of balance, with hardly any time to recover.

You see, given time, the Earth has a mechanism for restoring its balance. Right at the base of the Earth's mantle there is a mass of gooey stuff. Because it's so gooey it takes a long time to shift.

The normal forming and melting of glaciers is no problem. These processes take thousands of years.

But the suddenness of Lake Agassiz's emptying would have been a serious matter. It would have created a pretty big wobble, much bigger than 6 metres.

But how big?

This isn't a particularly easy question to answer. The problem is that we just don't know how the different layers of the Earth would have reacted. That's especially true of the 2,900-kilometre thick mantle, with its faults and lakes of liquid rock.

What we can do is make deductions based on the wobble that we have now. Then apply this to what might have happened in 6,250 BC.

But if I do this, then I find that the wobble would only have grown from 6 metres to about 100 metres – a long way short of the 400 miles that I need!

But hold on – I am scaling things up quite a lot here.

The imbalance due to Lake Agassiz's disappearance is some 100 times as large as that causing the wobble today.

Would the behaviour of the mantle still be the same with a wobble 100 times larger?

I am an engineer. I know that the materials I deal with change as they deform.

Take soil. A soil can change and become ten times less stiff when the amount that it deforms is multiplied by 100.

What if this applies to the Earth's mantle? It's not exactly a soil, but it isn't exactly solid either. It's full of cracks and faults.

And – no surprise – I find that if I assume a lower mantle stiffness, then I get a bigger wobble.

But only up to a point.

It doesn't matter how low I go; I can't predict a wobble of more than about a mile.

---

archaeology    geography ✓    creatures
science ✓    language    religion    folklore

**CHAPTER 9                A ROLLER-COASTER RIDE**

The problem is caused by something called the 'Coriolis Effect'. This is the effect that means it is difficult to turn a bicycle wheel when it is spinning.

When it is applied to the Earth it gives a reassuring level of stability.

I have to admit that when I got this far I nearly gave up. No matter how much I checked and re-checked everything, I could see no possibility of reaching a different conclusion.

And so far as I know, this is as far as anyone else has reached also.

But then, one day, I made a startling discovery. Accidentally, I used different properties for the mantle measured along the line of tilt, through Lake Agassiz, to those properties 90 degrees away. I was amazed at the result.

Instead of less than a mile of wobble, I found I had hundreds of miles of wobble. Suddenly, I had a prediction that could actually give a 300-metre flood. But could it be true?

I made my discovery by accident. Is there any reason to assume there really are different properties for different areas of the Earth's mantle? Well, maybe yes.

The major fault lines between the plates that make up the Earth's crust are called tectonic plates. If you look at a map of the Earth's tectonic plate boundaries, you will see they are not evenly distributed.

Near to the longitudes of what I have termed 'primary' tilt, through Lake Agassiz, approximately 90 degrees east and west, there are quite a lot of faults.

These lie through Central America, the eastern Pacific, northern India and the eastern Indian Ocean.

In contrast, there are fewer faults on the longitudes of 'secondary' tilt, induced through the Coriolis Effect, at approximately 0 degrees and 180 degrees of longitude.

The Pacific and African plates comprise large areas of relatively fault-free surface.

So, rightly or wrongly, I have formulated an equation. This assigns a mantle stiffness controlling 'primary' tilt which is approximately twice as great as that controlling 'secondary' tilt.

There's no way to prove or disprove it. All I can say is that it's reasonable. And it gives me the prediction shown in the following figure.

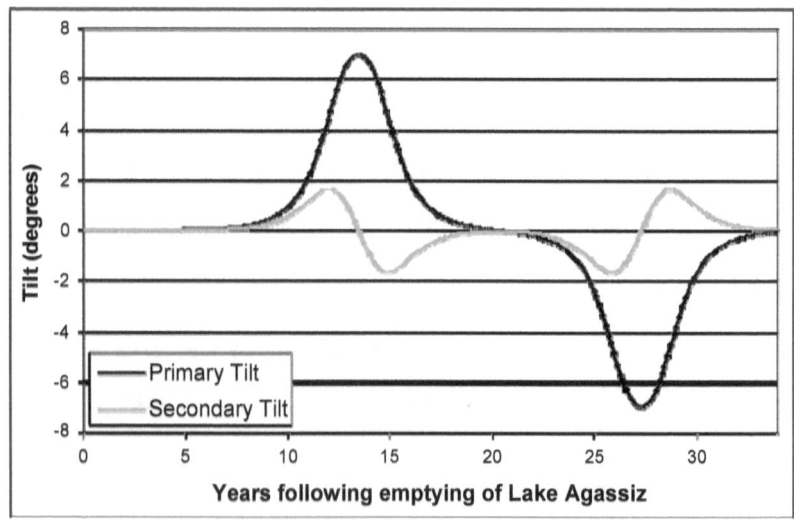

A tilt of nearly seven degrees equates to a 450-mile movement of the poles on the surface. With this amount of movement, I get a maximum rise in sea level, relative to the land, of about 440 metres. This is in middle latitudes on the line of 'primary' tilt.

These most unfortunate of locations are in North America, Central Asia, and parts of the southern Pacific and Indian oceans.

This rise in sea level reduces to a maximum of 100 metres on the line of 'secondary' tilt. There, it is 50 metres at the poles and no flood at all on the equator.

As you can see in the figure, two massive tilts are predicted, first one way then the other. This means that two quadrants of the Earth would be drowned first, while the other two saw the sea retreat. Then the situations would be reversed.

You could think of the whole thing as being like a roller-coaster journey.

A roller-coaster trundles slowly down the first gentle part of its run. The same happened for several years after Lake Agassiz emptied.

But then things began to speed up. It was as if the roller-coaster took a sudden dive down a really steep dip in the track.

Resistance built up as the mantle took the strain. This led to a slowing down and reversal of motion. It was like the roller-coaster reaching the bottom of a dip and then shooting up the next slope.

If you really were in a roller-coaster, you would know exactly what was coming next, however.

You would have a 'breather' for about a second at the top of the rise before you plunged headlong, once more, into another stomach-churning valley.

The Earth behaved in a similar manner.

It slowed as it regained its original position, but it had too much momentum. It kept going, and then speeded up again as it tilted the other way.

The same slowing down process happened again. Then the planet returned once more to its original position, slowing as it approached.

Now, however, the planet's built-in stabilisation system kicked in. There wasn't enough momentum to take it on a third tilt.

The result is that only the equator would have survived unscathed.

Everywhere else would have experienced sea level rise at some stage.

The next figure shows all the areas that are predicted to have been flooded, irrespective of when that flooding happened. You can see that North America and Central Asia would both have had a really rough time.

Areas flooded

Regarding the rate of increase, or decrease, of ocean level, middle latitudes would have experienced rates of no more than about half a metre per day.

Other locations would have seen even lower rates of water level rise.

So there would have been plenty of opportunity for escape, by humans or animals, so long as that escape was to sufficiently high ground.

But getting to high ground would be difficult in gently sloping, lowland regions. If there was no ground high enough, then escape may have been impossible without a boat.

By the way, you might be wondering if there is any danger of this kind of flood happening again – perhaps even soon.

Well, if my calculation is right, you would need to shift over 90% of the volume of water in Lake Agassiz to get the Earth to tilt in this dramatic way.

Anything less and the mantle would be stiff enough to return the planet to its rightful position with minimal fuss.

And as I look around the planet today, I simply cannot see any chance of this sort of thing happening.

There's no such water volume waiting to be released. It is hard to envisage any other mechanism that could possibly redistribute mass on this scale, over such a short time period.

I wouldn't want to give you the impression you were safe, but I would seriously doubt that mankind is in danger of another 'great flood'.

But is all this really to be believed?

We have a bunch of stories told by the ancients and a madcap theory about the Earth tilting!

Surely if this was all true, then we would have found evidence by now?

Well, let's look and see.

**CHAPTER 10        CLUES FROM ARCHAEOLOGY**

If this flood really happened, it was a long time ago.

In 6,250 BC most of mankind was living a hunter-gatherer existence, constantly on the move, not living in settlements. This is bad news for archaeologists. It means they find clues hard to come by.

But it's not all bad. Our ancestors made use of caves and rock shelters. We often find evidence of occupation in such places. In some parts of the world genuine houses and villages were being constructed.

Agriculture had already spread across the Middle East and was getting under way in China.

This meant that people had started to settle down for long periods in one place.

So we really ought to see some signs of this flood. And, in fact, we do.

Let me give you the comments of three archaeologists who have investigated different parts of the world. They all relate to this approximate time, 6,250 BC.

John Walthall compared two time periods in North American archaeology.

He spoke about the first half of the 7$^{th}$ millennium BC. At that time there was known to be a vigorously expanding population right across the eastern United States. He contrasted this with what he called the "little known, little studied" period that followed.

Kathleen Kenyon was the archaeologist who excavated Jericho during the 1950s and 1960s. She remarked on the end of a civilisation called 'Pre-pottery Neolithic B' with these words: "For some reason the light of progress seemed to flicker out."

Archaeologist R. K. Varma spoke about the abandonment of Mesolithic villages in the Ganges valley in India. He asked: "Where did the Mesolithic folk of the Ganges valley go? Where did they migrate to?"

The puzzle was the same in all three cases. It was the sudden disappearance of a thriving population living in a lowland location. In all three cases the date was around 6,250 BC.

Jericho lies about 250 metres below sea level in the Jordan valley. It would have taken at least 100 years for the flood waters to evaporate sufficiently for the city to emerge once more.

This ties in with the fact that it lay abandoned for some 500 years.

In Europe too, many archaeological sites display a gap in occupation around 6,250 BC.

This date roughly corresponds to the transition between Mesolithic and Neolithic cultures. It constitutes a serious puzzle to archaeologists.

Some archeological sites have been highlighted as showing a period of apparent lack of occupation. Some are listed here:

- Cyclops Cave on the Aegean island of Youra: 6,090-5,790 BC
- Theopetra's Cave, Greece: 6,650-5,880 BC
- Konispol's Cave, Albania: 6,310-6,080 BC
- Sidari, Corfu: 6,350-6,250 BC
- Corbeddu Cave, Sardinia: 6,250-5,850 BC
- La Poujade rock shelter, southern France: 6,650-6,030 BC

There are also gaps between Mesolithic and Neolithic layers at these locations:

- Dell'Uzzo Cave in Sicily
- Vercors in France
- Forcas, Botiquera, Costalena, and Margineda in Spain
- Franchthi Cave in southern Greece
- Odmut in Montenegro
- Vela Spila in Croatia

It is interesting that sites in the lower Ebro River valley in eastern Spain – including Forcas, Botiquera and Costalena – were abandoned abruptly around 6,250 BC and an archaeological gap followed. By contrast, sites further up-river seem to have been unaffected.

There is also an abrupt dip in the available dating records in southern France and north-eastern Spain during this exact period.

Mesolithic dates build to a peak around 6,250 BC and then fall away sharply. Neolithic dates are negligible until 6,050 BC and then rise rapidly to a peak in about 5,800 BC.

Whatever the reason, it is statistically significant.

---

| archaeology ✓ | geography | creatures |
| science | language | religion | folklore |

## CHAPTER 11    DRAMA ON THE PLAINS

Several of the sites show evidence of erosion or silting-up following the latest Mesolithic layers.

At La Digue, in the French Riviera, a one metre layer of sediment was found. This was between layers that showed the site to have been occupied. The sediment dated from around 6,350-6,150 BC.

In southern France, at Espeluche-Lalo on the Citelle River, and at Sidari in Corfu, there is more evidence. There is a significant amount of erosion that sliced away previous archaeological layers. At Sidari the date is also between 6,350 BC and 6,250 BC.

Many of the locations mentioned are on, or close to, the coast. The cause could have been a major invasion of the sea that destroyed these coastal sites.

Lepinski Vir in the Danube valley, in Serbia, is one of the best known Mesolithic archaeological sites in Europe.

Here, the Danube cuts through a narrow gorge at the southern extreme of the Carpathian Mountains. The area was in use from well before 8,000 BC.

Lepinski Vir is unusual for the time in Europe in that it was a settled village. There was genuine house construction.

This all changed in about 6,300 BC. The site, and others nearby, were abandoned and not re-occupied properly until about 5,950 BC.

Schela Chladovei, at the downstream mouth of that same gorge, is another interesting site. At around the same time there was a lot of sedimentation. This implies significant erosion upstream.

If a flood had indeed happened, that kind of erosion would have been inevitable. Water would have flowed at high-velocity through the gorge.

The site of Mehrgarh on the Bolan River in western Pakistan provides similar evidence. This was an early farming community. It underwent a sudden change at a date that is usually put at around 6,000 BC.

Here, too, a massive layer of silt has been found covering the site. It dates from this time.

Like the silt layer at Schela Chladovei on the Danube, this must certainly have been deposited underwater.

It would be difficult to imagine a more definite piece of evidence that a massive flood really did inundate that whole plain. I could go on and mention more examples:

- unexplained silt layers in Russian sites;
- the sudden end of the Sumnagin culture in the Russian Arctic;
- the lack of archaeology from south-east Asia in the centuries following 6,000 BC;

- the lack of Nile valley occupation between 6,000 BC and 5,200 BC, while development continued on the higher land on either side.

There are many, many more examples. The truth is that archaeologists right around the world know that something dramatic happened a bit before 6,000 BC. That 'something' really upset many different human societies.

This is usually blamed on climate change. Personally, I feel this is inadequate to explain such a remarkable series of events. Especially the fact that these disasters only seem to have struck low lying areas.

In India, normal development continued north and south of the Ganges plain. However, it ceased on the plain itself.

In the Middle East, Pre-pottery Neolithic B civilisation collapsed right across Palestine, parts of Syria and on Cyprus. Meanwhile, it kept going in the Jordanian hills.

There is an unexplained lack of cultural remains from the low lying Colorado Desert of southern California in the 7,000-5,000 BC time window. Contrast that with the continuous sequence found in the neighbouring, high altitude, Mojave Desert.

Basically, it's a pretty consistent picture – suspiciously consistent, I would say.

It begins to look as though the story of Noah could indeed have more than a foundation in truth. Plus those many other flood myths from around the world

But then, you might ask, wouldn't geologists or biologists have something to say? If the land, or the natural world had been under water for months, or years, wouldn't we notice some signs?

These are excellent and inescapable questions and in the next chapter I will have a go at answering them.

---

| archaeology | geography ✓ | creatures |
|---|---|---|
| science | language | religion | folklore |

**CHAPTER 12****CLUES FROM SCIENCE**

The first question to ask ourselves is: What would we expect to see in the way of evidence?

This was a slow, steady rise in water level. It was a non-violent event. So we wouldn't expect any actual change in the make-up of the land – unless the water had been forced to flow fast for some reason.

This was the case through the Danube gorge near Lepinsky Vir and Schela Chladovei.

In the natural world, even if vast numbers of animals and plants had perished, they would have recovered pretty quickly in most places.

There might be signs, such as a lack of species variety across flooded lands. Or the unexplained migration of species. However, these signs are likely to be rather vague and very hard to date.

So where to turn? I think the first place is sediments found on the beds of lakes.

Sediment analysis won't usually tell us about any change in the lake water itself. What it will tell us about are changes in the surrounding land.

The sediment in lakes varies according to surrounding soil types, vegetation, steepness of the land and amount of rainfall.

So, for example, if flooding killed all the vegetation, what we should see is a raised organic carbon content in the sediment.

We might also find evidence of increased land erosion, or a sudden change in pollen type or content.

Basically, any short-lived change to the sediment means a short-lived change to the surrounding area, which is exactly what a flood should produce.

I have found lake-bed data from 88 lakes and inland seas.

These lakes range from less than one square kilometer to very large. For example, the Baltic Sea, which in 6,250BC was a freshwater lake.

About a quarter of the lakes are 'closed'. They have no exit for the water. Three quarters are 'open'. They have a river running out of them.

Most importantly of all, they range from just above sea level to over 4,000 metres above sea level.

I have examined the data for each lake for changes that could plausibly be dated to about 6,250 BC. I have categorised these as:

- Sharp and short-lived
- Longer-lived, but reversed within a few hundred years
- Long-term

You can see the results in the next figure. This compares lakes where flooding is predicted with those above flood level. It also compares large and small lakes.

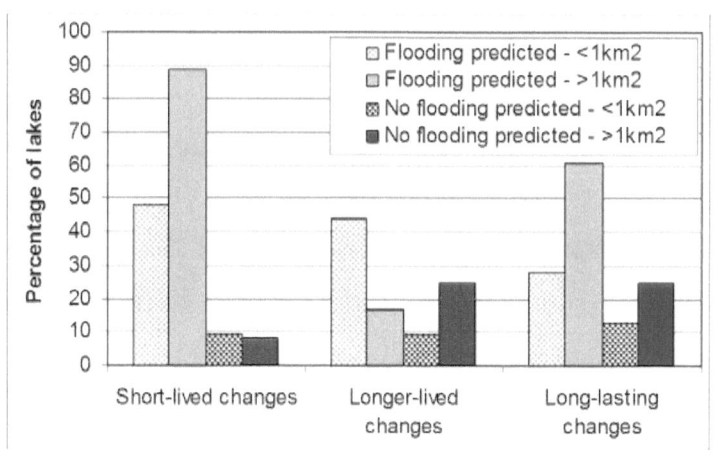

I hope you will agree that the results for short-lived changes are actually quite impressive.

The overwhelming majority of large lakes predicted to have been flooded show short-lived changes.

Many smaller lakes do, too. But here we would expect recovery to be very rapid, so signs would be harder to find.

In contrast, just a few lakes above the predicted flood level show such changes. This might be expected purely by coincidence.

For other types of change there is no clear distinction between flooded and non-flooded lakes.

But then, these are not the sorts of changes we are looking for. So pretty good results, I'd say.

It could all be coincidence I suppose. In that case you can add it to the long list of coincidences from archaeology. Personally, I feel that there are now so many coincidences that it is beginning to look a lot like proof!

The next figure illustrates these short-lived changes by plotting the TOC or 'total organic carbon' content in the sediment for eight lakes. Dating has been adjusted slightly in some cases – but dating is never accurate to less than 200-300 years.

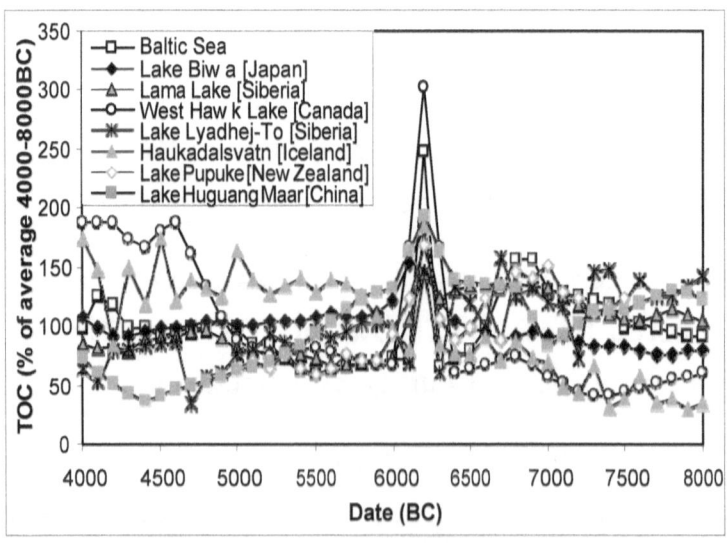

In most lakes, the salt water would have washed out in just a few years after the flood receded, leaving no trace. But, in very large lakes, we might expect to see something more.

Five of the largest are the American Great Lakes, which should all have been flooded. And the fact that something unusual happened in approximately 6,250 BC is abundantly clear.

---

    archaeology    geography    creatures
  science ✓    language    religion    folklore

## CHAPTER 13                 SALT IN THE WATER

We know something dramatic happened. This is because the remains of forests that show signs of sudden drowning have been discovered on the beds of Lake Huron and Lake Michigan.

Three metres of sediment have been reported around ancient tree stumps on the bed of southern Lake Michigan.

Intact clam shells were also found. This means they were buried rapidly. The remains of land beetles were also found. Chemical analysis of shells reveals a sudden change in water source.

But the most revealing geological signal is the sudden appearance of black, iron sulphide bands in sediments from this time.

They have been reported from all five great lakes, in each case commencing in roughly 6,250BC.

These bands unquestionably mean a lack of oxygen in the bottom water of the lake. Something must have occurred to prevent proper mixing of lake water. One known cause is where a layer of fresh water overlies salt water.

A massive influx of seawater would have done the job nicely!

Subsequent fresh water flowing in from rivers would be of lower density. It would therefore have tended to remain on the surface. Water lower down would still have been salty.

With time, the limited mixing that occurred would slowly have reduced the salt content of the bottom water. It could have taken several thousand years for this to happen.

The Caspian Sea is another very large lake where the water chemistry is surprisingly close to that of the ocean.

One recent estimate is that the difference

appears to have developed over only about 10,000 years. This view is totally incompatible with current understanding of Caspian Sea history.

The last time salt water is supposd to have penetrated the Caspian Sea was over 100,000 years ago.

I have carried out my own modelling of Caspian Sea chemistry. I find that it is entirely compatible with a salt water flood about 8,000 years ago.

Furthermore, the Caspian Sea is one of the few places where genuine biological evidence exists. It contains fourteen species that have arrived relatively recently from the Arctic.

They include fish, crustaceans, molluscs and the Caspian seal. A walrus tusk has even been discovered on the sea bed.

How on earth did these creatures get there? The Caspian Sea is more than 2,000 kilometres from the Arctic coastline.

While there is no shortage of theories on the subject, the simplest solution has not yet been discussed. It was probably a massive rise in sea level that brought Arctic water flowing across Siberia and straight into the Caspian Sea!

And how did 'Cardium edule', the common cockle, make the journey from the Black Sea to the Caspian Sea?

It appears in the sediment record shortly after 6,000BC. It just shouldn't be there. The standard explanation is that either a bird or a human was responsible for bringing it.

But it is hard to see how this could possibly have happened. It would have involved a journey of some 300 miles from the Black Sea to the Caspian Sea.

Yet again, this remarkable flood, which would have involved a flow of water from the Black Sea into the Caspian Sea, could provide the solution to an otherwise intractable problem.

Thinking about the Black Sea, however, brings me back to one of the popular explanations for Noah's flood. That is the so-called Black Sea flood, which I said earlier had been pretty much 'disproved' by scientists.

This 'disproving' consists of very strong evidence that at the date the flood was supposed to have happened, somewhere around 6,250 BC, the levels of the Black Sea and the Mediterranean were similar.

Given that fact, there would have been no reason for the Mediterranean to rush into the Black Sea.

On the other hand, studies of the floor of the narrow straits of both the Bosphorus and the Dardanelles reveal that massive erosion did indeed take place some time before 5,400 BC.

This erosion removed between 20 and 40 metres of sediment from both channels, down to basement level rock. This could only be due to very high volumes of very fast water flowing through.

There is also evidence of a massive flow through what is called the 'Manych spillway'. This is an ancient channel that in times past used to connect the Black Sea and the Caspian Sea.

So, despite being impossible in the view of most scientists, it looks like some sort of Black Sea flood happened after all!

But how could it?

---

   archaeology     geography     creatures ✓
science ✓   language     religion     folklore

## CHAPTER 14                THE YANGTZE GORGE

The only possible mechanism is if the level of the Mediterranean rose temporarily far above its normal state.

This would have set up tremendous cascades of water through these straits and channels.

Like it or not, the Black Sea evidence goes a long way towards proving that this flood actually took place!

We are lucky to have this evidence. There aren't many places in the world where narrow channels like the Bosphorus and the Dardanelles exist.

They would have turned a non-violent event into something that, locally, would have been very violent indeed.

There are just two more that I can think of. One is the Danube gorge (known as the Iron Gates) where we have already found a nice big silt deposit at Schela Chladovei.

The other is the Yangtze gorge where China has recently been constructing a series of massive dams.

Here, I believe, we can look once more to the evidence of folk history.

The ancient Chinese tale of Yu tells the story of a man who was given the task of draining the land after it has been devastated by a great flood. This required the excavation of channels so that the water could return to the sea. The task took 13 years. Here is one version of the story, or at least part of it:


"The inundating waters seemed to assail the heavens, and in their extent embraced the hills and overtopped the great mounds so that the people were bewildered and overwhelmed.

I opened passages for the streams throughout the nine provinces and conducted them to the seas. I deepened the channels and conducted them to the streams."

Okay, it's another flood story. But why should it have been necessary to help the water reach the sea? And where was ancestral Chinese culture in 6,250 BC anyway?

I am confident that the answer to this question is in the middle reaches of the Yangtze river.

I am not alone in finding that ancestral Chinese language arrived via the Yangtze from India. In 6,250 BC it was beginning to spill out from the Yangtze gorge across the plain of central China. This was the exact region where rice agriculture had recently begun to take hold.

Assuming that the story of Yu is indeed an original Chinese tale, it may also derive from this time and place. And in the context of the Yangtze gorge, the story makes perfect sense.

The rush of water through the gorge, to and from the Sichuan plain to the west, would have caused plenty of erosion. This would surely have dammed the river. Once the flood had retreated, it would have prevented proper drainage of the land. It's not exactly hard evidence – but it all ties in.

So, we have checked out lake bed evidence. We have looked more closely at some very large lakes and inland seas. We have considered the channels where rapid flow would have taken place.

Perhaps I should mention the Dead Sea at this point.

The Dead Sea is below sea level. In the Dead Sea a massive layer of salt has been found in deposits on the sea floor. They date to some time between 5,000 and 9,000 BC.

This is exactly what we would expect if the whole valley of the Jordan had been filled with sea water and then left to evaporate.

Interestingly, the Dead Sea deposits also show two much earlier layers, dating from about 200,000 and 420,000 years ago. These suggest that the flood of 6,250 BC may not have been the only one of its kind, if you look back far enough.

Both these dates tie in approximately with the ends of earlier ice ages, which means that the same thing might well have happened then as in 6,250 BC.

This supports evidence from the Qattara Depression in Egypt. This is also below sea level. Successive terraces can be seen, suggesting repeated flooding by sea water, followed by evaporation and wind erosion over a period of up to two million years.

## CHAPTER 15            THE BAIKAL SEAL

We know several species inexplicably crossed the impassably cold Arctic Ocean. These offer evidence of repeated floods, from the point of view of biology.

'Phycodris rubens', a red alga, 'Mytilus trossulis', the blue mussel and 'Macoma balthica', a snail species, all crossed the Arctic from the Pacific to the North Atlantic some time within the last 15,000 years.

In the case of 'Macoma balthica' there have been four separate crossings over the last two million years.

If this sort of flood took place, it would have forced relatively warm water into the Arctic from both the Pacific and the Atlantic.

This would have acted as the sudden opening of a long-closed door.

Without this exceptional warming, it is hard to see how movement of these species could possibly have taken place.

Then there is the strange case of the Baikal seal. How could an ancestral seal pair have made the 2,000-mile cross-country journey from the Arctic Ocean to Lake Baikal?

Seals normally live in the ocean and they just don't do that sort of thing!

Yet the flood would have brought the Arctic right up the valley of the Angara river, to within a few miles of the lake. It would have brought all manner of Arctic wildlife with it, including seals.

When the flood retreated, some of these seals may have been stranded and then wandered up-river to Lake Baikal.

Like the Caspian seal, the Baikal seal is closely related to the Arctic ringed seal. Estimates for the date of its separation from a common ancestor range from 400,000 to 2 million years.

If approximately 400,000 years is correct, then this ties in with the flood that led to one of the salt deposits beneath the Dead Sea. Without such a flood, the Baikal Seal remains an intractable mystery.

And if this flood could lift seals up over 400 metres, then it would have done the same to ice sheets and coastal glaciers, in the Arctic and Antarctic.

This would have created a veritable plague of icebergs!

Of course, icebergs melt and leave no direct evidence. Actually, they are never one hundred per cent ice. They contain particles of grit picked up by the glaciers that formed the icebergs.

When the icebergs melt, these grit particles fall to the seabed and can be seen in the sediment.

So it's nice to learn that samples taken from the Norwegian Sea tell a story. They show a sudden, short-lived, twenty-fold increase in grit content in approximately 6,000 BC.

We also see less well dated evidence off the coast of Antarctica. There was a complete break up of both the Amery ice shelf and the George the Sixth ice shelf. Both then reformed over the course of several hundred years.

In the case of the George the Sixth ice shelf, the evidence is particularly clear. It consists of a thick layer of debris followed by several hundred years of sediment. This is typical of open water conditions.

We also have remarkable evidence that the largest ice shelf of all, the Ross ice shelf, was phyisically lifted from its bed. This caused oxygenated water to be sucked into the gap between the ice and the sea bed. This then led to iron-staining of the sea bed.

The iron-staining proves that oxygenated water got there. The question is, how? The flood provides the answer.

So I hope you can begin to see that this flood is much more than a crackpot theory about the Earth wobbling and a set of dubious myths!

There really is sound scientific evidence.

Accurate dating of the various events I have described has often been difficult. Many of the dates given are approximate.

However, the final clue that I will mention actually has the potential to date the flood very precisely indeed. It comes from tree rings.

Very few mature European oak tree specimens have been found in river deposits dating from 6,250 BC to 5,950 BC. In any given year in the centuries before and after, typically around fifty trees were found.

The implication is that a 'cull' of mature oaks took place around this time for some reason.

Submersion in sea water provides reason enough!

---

archaeology   geography   creatures ✓
science ✓ language   religion   folklore

**CHAPTER 16                THE GARDEN OF EDEN**

It is time to return to Noah. The question here is: How does Noah's flood match what we now know to be reality?

It is not stated anywhere just where Noah lived. However, the Bible does tell us about the Garden of Eden. This is the place where Noah's distant ancestors, Adam and Eve, are said to have lived.

For a start, since 'Eden' is the Sumerian word for 'plain', this strongly suggests that Eden lay somewhere out on the plains of Iraq.

The Bible reports that four rivers then converged in Eden. They are the Tigris, the Euphrates, the Gihon and the Pishon. The Tigris and Euphrates we know well enough – although not the exact route they took across the Iraqi plain in 6,250 BC.

The Pishon is said to have flowed through the land of Havilah. The name 'Havilah' may plausibly be identified with the River 'Hawrah'. This flows into the Euphrates in central Iraq.

The Gihon is said to have flowed through the land of Cush. This may well be an ancient name for the Zagros Mountains, known in Persian as 'Kuhha'.

From these clues we can assume that the approximate position of Eden was probably somewhere in central Iraq. Noah may therefore have lived not too far away.

According to the Bible, the flood arrived on the 17$^{th}$ day of the 2$^{nd}$ month. According to our present calendar that would be early May. It reports that the waters flooded the land for 150 days.

The ark cleared the tops of the mountains by 20 feet (15 cubits). So far as Noah was aware, during this five month period, the keel (or perhaps the sea anchor) never made contact with any land.

The ark is reported to have run aground five months later on the 17$^{th}$ day of the 7$^{th}$ month. Logically, this should have happened at around the high point of the flood. If the ark had grounded any earlier, rising waters would inevitably have refloated it.

Assuming this to be the case, and taking five months as an accurate record, this means that Noah must have entered his ark when the water was already within 20-25 metres of its maximum level.

In central Iraq this would mean an elevation of about 265-270 metres above sea level.

If this is true, then it narrows down the range of possible locations considerably. Most of the Iraqi plain lies at much lower elevations.

It forces us to look at a particular range of low hills that extend either side of the River Tigris. These hills would have formed natural refuges to which the inhabitants of the plain would have retreated as the water level rose.

As the water deepened they would have formed a small group of islands in a sea that otherwise stretched from horizon to horizon. This would have been a logical launching point for an ark.

As the flood rose still higher, most of these islands would eventually have been entirely covered with water.

This proposed location can only be a guess. If the duration given in the Bible is wrong, then this location may also be wrong. Nevertheless it seems to fit reasonably well.

It is not far from the settlement of Jarmo, which was a local centre of agricultural development.

It is also not too far from the region of central Iraq which the Bible implies as the location of the Garden of Eden.

---

|  archaeology | geography | creatures |
|  science | language | religion ✓ folklore |

## CHAPTER 17                   NOAH'S DILEMMA

Whether we speak of Noah, or the head of another household elsewhere, the dilemma would have been the same.

With an ever-shrinking patch of dry land, an agonising decision had to be made. Should they venture out onto the sea, or hope that the waters would stop their relentless advance before everyone drowned.

That would have been the scenario that was played out in many places the world over.

It's just that in this particular location, an individual whose neighbours probably considered him quite mad, had already built a giant boat.

But where exactly was it that the ark grounded, some five months later?

The location given in the Bible is the mountains of Ararat. I said in Chapter 1 this should really be rendered 'mountains of Urartu'.

During the period of history when the majority of the so-called Old Testament of the Bible was compiled, Urartu was the name of the country north of the Tigris plain.

However, I think we can be a little more specific about Noah's landfall. The Koran reports that the ark landed on a certain Mount Judi.

It just so happens that there is a Mount Judi. It is a little north of the Tigris River, on the edge of the mountains of Urartu. That is right on the predicted shoreline of the flood.

The location is exactly where it should be. If the winds were from the south, this would have driven Noah and his ark into one of the northern inlets.

The lower slopes of Mount Judi would therefore be one of the most likely locations for the ark to come to rest.

It was most probably accompanied by all manner of flotsam and jetsam from the homes and businesses of those who had perished across the flooded plain.

The Bible tells us next that the tops of the mountains became visible on the $1^{st}$ day of the $10^{th}$ month. That would be about 10 weeks after first running aground.

According to the prediction, the water level would only have fallen by about 3-5 metres from its peak by then.

But I guess it's quite possible that this was enough for the rocks at the tops of one or more adjacent hills to have appeared in view, as Noah and his family looked out of their porthole.

The story seems to imply that they could only see out across the flooded valley of the Tigris. They couldn't see the other way, where Mount Judi would have risen behind them.

There then followed two months during which Noah is supposed to have released first a raven and then a dove. This was to check whether there was enough solid ground for him and his family to live on.

Eventually, some time in early March, with the flood now 15 metres below the high water mark, the dove returned with an olive leaf in its beak.

Noah knew that plants were sprouting once more. Then he could at last remove the covering from the ark.

He was a cautious man, however. And, let's face it, he'd had a rather traumatic experience.

So he and his family only left the ark on the 27$^{th}$ day of the 2$^{nd}$ month. That was just over a year after climbing aboard.

At that point the water level should have lowered by about 25-30 metres.

The whole plain was still flooded, of course, but at least the water was going the right way – down!

Basically, it all makes pretty good sense.

The statement that all the creatures on the face of the earth perished is entirely accurate. You need to appreciate that the 'earth' refers not to the entire planet, but rather the earth known by

Noah. The 'earth' he knew was the plains of northern Iraq.

The reference to all the high mountains is to the hills that Noah was familiar with. That's what he saw vanishing beneath the rising water. It doesn't refer to the Himalayas or the Andes, of which he had no knowledge.

The bottom line is that this particular flood myth, unlike some others from across the globe, may well be true. And true not only in essence, but also in detail – and that is remarkable indeed.

**Word meanings:**

**Crustaceans** – lobsters, crabs, shrimps etc

**Cuneiform** – earliest form of writing

**Erosion** – wearing away of soil and rock

**Magma** – red-hot liquid rock

**Mantle** – layer between the earth's crust and its inner core

**Molluscs** – shellfish such as cockles and mussels

**Momentum** – forward movement

**Mortar** – big bowl

**Sediment** – mud, earth and plant debris in water

**Silting** – filling with mud

**Subterranean** – below the earth's surface

**Tectonic plates** – massive sections of the earth's crust that move slightly and collide

**Tsunami** – tidal wave

'The Man on the Mountain Top' is based on a much longer book by Nick Thom entitled 'The Great Flood' (2$^{nd}$ Edition), Grosvenor House Publishing, 2011, ISBN 978-1-908596-86-4

www.ingramcontent.com/pod-product-compliance
Lightning Source LLC
Chambersburg PA
CBHW021116080526
44587CB00010B/536